LEADERSHIP

20 Successful Tips On How to Become a True Leader Who Inspires Everyone and Creates Profound Visions That Lead to Progress

By CARRIE DRESDEN

Table of Contents

Introduction

Leaders come in many varieties. Some leaders are outgoing and enthusiastic, while others are subdued and authoritative. The best leaders share a talent for inspiration, regardless of personal style. True leaders, the kind who inspire everyone around them, are those who create profound visions and are able to communicate those visions to others. This ability is crucial for leaders of all kinds: entrepreneurs, business owners, office managers, civic and religious leaders, school administrators, and more. If you have a desire to improve your leadership skill, whether you lead a team of 1 or 100, this book will guide you to greater success.

The 20 successful tips included in this book will take you through the step-by-step process of becoming a better, more inspirational leader. At the conclusion of each leadership, tip is a thought-provoking question. Taking the time to consider these questions will further increase your understanding of leadership and inspiration. Additionally, each tip includes an action step: something you can implement immediately in your project or workplace to create profound visions that lead to progress.

These tips are designed to build upon each other, but can be read in any order. After you work your way through the book, you may find yourself going back to certain portions again and again. The skills and procedures of a successful leader are timeless. Igniting your passion and improving your ability to inspire others can become a life-long pursuit that brings about greater success and fulfillment.

Chapter 1: Start with Yourself

The best leaders know that before they can inspire those around them, they must first inspire themselves. Use the tips in this chapter to make the most of your talents and further refine your profound vision.

Tip #1: Acknowledge Your Fears

All leaders, no matter how talented, have fears. It is not the existence of fear that is the problem, however. The difficulty comes when fear of failure or rejection halts progress and stifles inspiration. One way to move forward in spite of fear is to first acknowledge it. Next, find a way to reduce your fear's control of the situation. This can range from asking advice from someone you respect that has successfully navigated a similar situation to planning for contingencies in the project. You may not eliminate the fear altogether, but being better prepared will allow you to succeed nonetheless.

Many times, fears come from new experiences. The first sales pitch is undoubtedly more nerve-racking than the thirty-first. Plan to do the thing that scares you as soon as possible. Once you have one successful attempt under your belt, you can hone your skill and move forward with confidence.

Even after greater preparation and practice, you will experience some failure. True leaders recognize that any worthy goal is worth that risk. Learning from failure is as important in your growth as a leader as conquering fear. Committing to trying something new, even if you might fail, opens the door to greater creativity. Having the courage to accept potential failure allows you to attempt things you might otherwise avoid. Not all of those attempts will be successful, but some of them will.

> ➤ Question for Thought: What fear is keeping you from your leadership potential?

> ➤ Action Step: Practice something you fear in front of a friend.

Tip #2: Always Have a Book (or Two) Nearby

Many world-class leaders have documented what led to their successes in everything from biographies to how-to books. Reading gives you the opportunity to learn from successful leaders and apply their hard-earned experience to your own goals and vision. Although nothing can substitute for hands-on experience, reading about the journey of other leaders will give you the next best thing. Rather than repeat the same beginner mistakes, you can move forward knowing what to anticipate. Books on time management, communication, marketing, or entrepreneurship can provide concrete suggestions for improving productivity. More specific books about technology and industry techniques can expand your skill set. In addition to nuts-and-bolts information, leaders also gain inspiration from others through books. Reading accounts of passion and success will recharge your motivation.

Make it a habit to always be working through a book. While it may feel like you do not have time to add reading to your long list of daily chores and tasks, the effort will pay off in greater of focus, inspiration, and knowledge. Many highly recommended books on leadership and best practices are available in audio form as well. Reading a few pages a day or using commute and exercise time to listen to a book will have a dramatic effect on your overall confidence and ability.

➢ Question for Thought: Who is a well-known leader you admire?

➢ Action Step: Identify five books on leadership, inspiration, or best practices you would like to read this year. Consider a book by or about the leader you identified earlier.

Tip #3: Identify the Best and Emulate Them

True leaders who inspire lasting progress learn from each other. Identify two or three examples of success and learn everything you can from their experiences. The more you learn about those who have achieved what you are working toward, the more you will be able to emulate their success. Do not limit yourself to leaders in your field alone. There are many great public speakers, for example, that may be in a line of work very different from your own. Sales and marketing strategies can improve fundraising efforts for non-profit organizations, even if the application differs. You will gain valuable insight from successful leaders who display traits you would like to develop, no matter the specific industry.

Learning from those you admire can take the form of in-person mentorship. Mentoring, at its best, stems from a relationship of mutual trust, but it does not need to be a long-term commitment. Just meeting once for lunch with someone whose opinion you respect is an opportunity to learn to achieve similar success or avoid similar mistakes.

As mentioned in the previous tip, reading books about, and by, successful leaders will give you a glimpse into their experiences as well. Many current experts in leadership and business regularly publish articles online.

➤ Question for Thought: If you could have one hour with a leader you admire, what questions would you ask?

➤ Action Step: Brainstorm a list of 3-4 people whose opinion you respect.

Tip #4: Learn Something New Every Day

No matter how much experience or education you have currently, there is always something new you can learn. Many industries are changing so rapidly, even a specialized training only stays relevant for a short time. To inspire lasting progress, a leader must be able to learn and adapt constantly. Ever-changing technology, demographics, and trends demand leaders that can modify their practices quickly. Never before has there been such a vast amount of information available at the push of a button, but a leader must be able to discern which information sources are most valuable. Finding up-to-date information is critical in staying abreast of these changes.

In addition to work-related knowledge, the simple act of learning keeps your mind nimble. Learning a new skill unrelated to work can increase your confidence and creativity. Improving your posture or vocabulary, though not directly related to the bottom line, will have a positive effect on your ability to inspire others. A commitment to lifelong learning will help you face the ever-changing demands of leadership.

➢ Question for Thought: How does learning prepare you for leadership?

➢ Action Step: Learn something new today.

Chapter 2: Set the Stage

Once you have prepared yourself to be a more effective leader, you are ready to expand your circle of influence to those around you. Building a solid foundation of motivated personnel and high expectations will greater increase your chance for success.

Tip #5: Build the Right Team

Avoid the temptation to hire the first qualified applicant just for the sake of speed. Many expensive setbacks will be avoided by hiring slowly. Take enough time to seek out those who truly share the vision behind your company or project. Your team will be more successful if everyone from the bottom up is committed to the goal. Another added bonus is that you will have less employee turnover, which will save you valuable time and money. Filling empty positions is time-consuming and expensive. Frequent turnover can halt progress and degrade morale. Spending the time to find the right person the first time will prevent costly interruptions down the road.

Once you have your team members selected, make sure that each one is using his or her talents in the best way. Successful leaders recognize the skills that each team member possesses and direct those skills accordingly. Not all workers have the same talents or interests, so everyone will be happier and more productive if the right people fill the right roles. It may take some work to find where every person belongs, but it will be worth the effort. Use performance evaluations to get an idea of where a particular team member will excel. If you are still unsure, meet with the employee in question and ask for input.

> ➤ Question for Thought: Have you ever seen the negative effects of hiring too quickly?

> ➤ Action Step: Enlist the help of your current team to locate the right talent. If those on your team are passionate about the mission, they will be connected to others with similar motivations.

Tip #6: Set Clear Expectations and Ambitious Goals

Even the most motivated team member will have difficulty being successful without a clear picture of what is expected. Communicating specific performance expectations is a great way to make sure that the progress being made fits properly within the vision. Providing clear expectations and measurable goals will help keep your team on track. It also becomes easier to pinpoint those who are ready for more responsibility and those who are not keeping up.

Start first with each member of your team. Do they know what success looks like in their specific roles? Evaluate any existing job descriptions and refine them if needed. A detailed outline of what is expected of each team member will provide a clear framework for any performance evaluation. Employees will know when they are meeting expectations and so will you.

Progress requires both powerful inspiration and practical progress toward a goal. Once your team understands the importance of your vision, spend some time working on how to achieve success. Set specific and measurable goals with your team. Allowing team members to be involved in the goal-setting process will help them feel valued. That sense of ownership will translate to initiative in accomplishing their goals. Another trait of a true leader is stretching the team's potential. Encourage your team to set ambitious goals.

Make time to regularly assess your team's progress. Once you have clear expectations in place, the evaluations will be more straightforward and efficient. Provide encouragement and clarity where needed. When your team reaches their goal, take the time to celebrate with them. After acknowledging and celebrating the success, they will be motivated to set another ambitious goal.

➤ Question for Thought: What goals are you working on right now? Are they written down?

➤ Action Step: Create a specific job description for yourself or someone in the company. Be sure to enumerate what success looks like in that specific position. Request feedback and revise if necessary.

Tip #7: Foster Respect by Developing Talent

Investing time in employees will go a long way to keeping you from having to replace them. Inspiring leaders are willing to mentor team members and pass on knowledge gained. This simple act will build rapport, enhance workplace morale, and ultimately develop the skills of the team. An environment that nurtures trust and development will foster a culture of growth and confidence. Recognizing interests and talents in your team members and using your experiences to encourage growth is a sign of a generous leader.

In the beginning, you may need to spend more time supervising projects. As individuals demonstrate they are capable and trustworthy, you can allow more autonomy. If you find the team member making mistakes, you may have given too much freedom too quickly. Enumerate to the employee what you would like to see differently and stay more involved in the process the next time.

Inspiring leaders expand their mentoring beyond work-related training. Showing a genuine interest in your team members will show them that you are committed to helping them improve in all areas of their lives. They will respond with loyalty and enthusiasm. This environment of mutual respect will contribute to lasting change.

> ➤ Question for Thought: What experiences can you use to train a leader on your team?

> ➤ Action Step: Identify someone on your team who has a skill you can nurture.

Tip #8: Communicate the Vision

Effective leaders develop a clear vision of where the project or company is going and communicate it to the team. This is one of the most important aspects of inspirational leadership. The most successful leaders are able to vividly articulate why their product or idea matters.

The use of metaphor can be a powerful tool in describing the vision. Painting a picture for your team of why they, and others, should care about what you do will help guide all decisions and progress. All members of your team should be able to answer the following questions: Why does what we do matter? Who does it help? How do we provide this service?

Use details and description to get your team to better understand the vision. Connecting to people's emotions will make a more powerful vision that lasts. Every single decision and expectation should tie back to the company vision. The clearer the vision, the more inspired the team will be in their work.

> ➤ Question for Thought: What is your mission? Why does it matter?

> ➤ Action Step: Articulate the vision to your team.

Chapter 3: Keep At It

Presenting a profound vision is just the first step to successful leadership. Now that you have your team and vision in place, keep working. This chapter will cover strategies to prevent problems from arising and the best way to handle them if they do. Day-to-day dedication to the vision is what leads to further progress.

Tip #9: Make Decisions, then Own Them

Successful leaders use their time wisely, and that includes time spent on decisions. Act decisively and then take responsibility for the result. If something goes wrong, own up to it. Then use the failure as a chance to modify your practices accordingly. When things go well, take note of what contributed to the success. This will set an example for your team as well. True leaders understand that their actions dictate the standard of behavior more than their words.

This does not mean you must make decisions alone. Successful leaders respect input from the team. Set aside a specific amount of time to consider all aspects of the decision and invite feedback. Once the discussion period has ended, make the best decision available. When your team members feel included in the decision, they will work harder for its success.

➤ Question for Thought: Which part of making decisions is more difficult for you: seeking input or being decisive?

➤ Action Step: Find an aspect of your project that is waiting on a decision. Set a time frame for how long you will consider the options, and then move forward.

Tip #10: Earn Respect by Demonstrating Integrity

True leaders are honest and keep promises. Colleagues and customers are more likely to have confidence in the ideas of a leader who has demonstrated integrity. It will take time for you to establish yourself as a person of integrity, but the benefit is worth the effort. When those around you see your commitment to integrity, they will be more inspired by the things you say because your words will have the weight of your consistent action as well.

Effective workplaces involve respect at all levels. The ability to trust employees is paramount when giving responsibilities and allowing access to sensitive material or resources. A culture of honesty and trustworthiness starts at the very top. Successful leaders are intentional about what they do and say because they know those they lead will be watching for inconsistencies.

The belief system that directs the leader is the driving force behind decisions, employee retention, and motivation at all levels of the company. A detailed vision has only limited motivational potential without the respect of your team. A true leader inspires others to make lasting change by setting an example of honesty and authenticity.

> ➤ Question for Thought: How does integrity engender respect?

> ➤ Action Step: Keep your promises. If you have been less-than-honest previously, be candid about your mistakes and commitment to change.

Tip #11: Address Problems Promptly

No matter how carefully a leader has made hiring decisions and articulated the vision, challenges inevitably arise. Whether in the form of a team member who is not contributing, a disagreement with a client, or a downturn in the economy, there are setbacks in every journey. True leaders know that ignoring challenges only allows them to grow. Instead of avoiding or putting off uncomfortable situations, face them head-on. Naming the problem and confronting it eliminates the tendency for unaddressed challenges to seem worse than they really are. This decisiveness will reassure your team that you are committed to the project and to them.

Use difficulties as a chance to gain knowledge and improve your strategy. Once resolved, you can use the experience to lessen the chances of the same problem cropping up again. Evaluate what contributed to the problem and implement a plan to remove the factors in the future. Even for difficulties outside your control, you will have practice for the next time something similar interferes with progress.

> ➢ Question for Thought: What happens to productivity when a problem is allowed to fester?

> ➢ Action Step: Evaluate your project and identify any problems you may have been avoiding.

Chapter 4: Be a Generous Leader

A generous leader is one that inspires loyalty and dedication. Generosity is a sign of confidence and security. Building up others with your generosity will ensure that the changes you make will last.

Tip #12: Be Generous with Praise

Letting your team know when they have done something right has an amazing impact on their confidence and enthusiasm. A feeling of shared success and buy-in motivates all team members going forward. Rather than leading to complacency, appreciation actually increases productivity. When you are quick to notice success or innovation, it will encourage your team members to keep at it.

The opposite of praise is a complaint. Discourage gossip and criticism in the workplace. It is all too easy for employees to turn to gossip and blame, which hurt morale and productivity. Make it clear that problems will be addressed fairly rather than complained about and that idle discussion about who said or did what is not welcome. When you, as the leader, are direct with your corrections and generous with well-earned praise, your team will follow suit.

➢ Question for Thought: How do you feel when someone recognizes the hard work you do?

➢ Action Step: Say thank you to someone on your team. Tell him or her specifically what you are grateful for and what impact it had on the project.

Tip #13: Reward Creativity and Support Autonomy

Encourage team members to develop expertise in areas that do not come naturally to you. Each individual will bring a separate skill set to the table. Fostering individual talents will bring skills to your team that it may currently lack. The more confidence and expertise your team have, the more they will be able to bring your vision to life. Employees will be more dedicated to work in which they feel a sense of ownership. By turning the work from your personal project to a group endeavor, you will support autonomy and buy-in from your team. You will find that they begin to care why their work matters and how it fits in with the overall vision. Another benefit of a confident, involved team is that you will be able to trust them with incrementally more and more responsibility. This leaves you free to focus on long-term goals.

Part of inspiring lasting change is retaining employees who understand your profound vision. Replacing employees is expensive and requires time, both in hiring and training. Some companies are finding they retain more employees by offering more flex time or the option to work remotely on occasion. Even in situations when this is not practical, a successful leader encourages the team to feel responsible for a project by allowing flexibility in how the goal is reached. By establishing a profound vision of *why* the goal is important and articulating *what* success will look like, your team can confidently arrange the details in any number of way. This sort of freedom increases intrinsic motivation and productivity.

Similarly, rewarding creativity will keep your team from becoming complacent. A successful leader inspires others so effectively that they understand why the goal is important and take pride in a job well done.

- ➢ Question for Thought: How do you encourage creativity?

- ➢ Action Step: Find a way to give greater autonomy to your team.

Tip #14: Keep Lines of Communication Open

"No news is good news" has no place in leadership. Make it a point to communicate with your team regularly. This can be accomplished by clarifying objectives, providing updates on progress, further developing the company vision, or welcoming feedback. Establishing a habit of regular communication will keep small problems from escalating due to neglect. Address setbacks or problems directly, but do not let that be the only time you communicate with your team.

Communicating optimism promotes faith and confidence in the team. True leaders inspire lasting progress by tapping into the emotions and motivations of those around them. Reminding your team why the project matters and the positive outcomes achieved to date will generate more enthusiasm.

➢ Question for Thought: How can you communicate optimism to those you lead?

➢ Action Step: If you do not have one already, schedule a regular time for team meetings. Keep the meetings brief. Focus on the profound vision you have for the company.

Chapter 5: Keep Moving Forward

Even poor leaders have periods of success; the key to becoming a great leader is achieving *consistent* success over time. Translating passion to long-term progress requires both motivation and flexibility. A combination of both, as outlined in this chapter, will help you make your progress last.

Tip #15: Keep the Vision Accessible

It is not enough to articulate the vision to the team only once. No matter how powerful the introduction of the company's mission, successful leaders will find multiple ways to keep the vision in the forefront of everything they do. Returning again and again to your vision will foster a unified purpose among your team. Refer to the vision when communicating with your team, especially via multiple channels of communication. Specifically, refer to why the vision matters in day-to-day emails, phone calls, and in-person meetings. An inspiring leader supports the vision with his or her actions. Your commitment to the mission will serve as a visible reminder.

In addition to referencing the vision, put it in writing. Enlist the help of your team to come up with a memorable visual representation. You will know that the message is getting across to your team when discussion of the vision happens organically. Lasting change will not occur until the profound vision permeates the daily decision making of your team.

> ➤ Question for Thought: When was the last time you presented your vision to someone one-on-one?

> ➤ Action Step: Write down the vision and put it in a visible location.

Tip #16: Report Success with Stories of Real People

An employee that is motivated by more than a paycheck will always work better and harder toward a goal. One important way to inspire this sense of purpose in your team members is to give examples of the good that is coming from their work. Use stories of real people to regularly show your team the benefit of their success. The more you can paint a complete picture of the lives improved by their work, the more dedication your team will put toward the project.

Even if you think that your work is not inspiring, think again. The goal might be a certain amount of growth or sales, but that is the *what* of the work, not the *why*. The *why* of your work likely has, at least, two main groups of beneficiaries: customers and employees. The immediate benefit of the work might be greater financial security for your customers and job stability for your employees. There are undoubtedly stories of lives improved by those seemingly mundane benefits. Successful leaders inspire by focusing on who is helped by the work being done.

> ➢ Question for Thought: Why does your work matter?

> ➢ Action Step: Make a list of real people whose lives are improved by the work you do. Jot down specific details that come to mind that could be part of the overall picture you paint for your team.

Tip #17: Welcome Feedback

The most successful leaders are always looking for new ways to improve themselves and their product. Employees that are invested in the work will undoubtedly be able to see things that you cannot. Solicit suggestions from your team. When they see that you are sincere in welcoming feedback, they will respond. This is yet another way to keep communication positive and consistent.

If you have not yet developed the optimal level of trust and communication with your team, invite their feedback anyway. Because some employees may fear termination if they give critical feedback, consider a method for submitting feedback anonymously. When your team sees you respond positively to suggestions, you will build an environment where honest suggestions can be given and received openly.

Even if a suggestion does not fit with the direction or scope you choose to take the company, acknowledge the idea and thank the person presenting it. Not only will you discover great ideas, but also you will be empowering your team. When they see that you are serious about listening to their ideas, they will be more creative and inspired. They will keep coming up with better ways to do things if they feel their suggestions are heard.

➢ Question for Thought: What is the best idea you have heard recently?

➢ Action Step: Set aside a regular time for team members to pitch ideas.

Chapter 6: Start With Yourself (Again)

Just as leaders must first inspire themselves, leaders must also take care of themselves. This chapter will focus on what you can do to keep yourself enthusiastic and on the forefront of progress.

Tip #18: Avoid Burnout

Leadership inherently comes with stress and criticism. Effective leaders maintain the necessary emotional resiliency because they seek peace and rest. Be mindful of your own emotions. Avoid a debilitating spiral of panic and inefficiency by creating a routine of recharging activities. Make time for daily exercise or meditation. Take periodic breaks from work at your desk by taking a walk, getting a drink of water, or encouraging team members. You will find that you are more efficient and focused if you take short breaks throughout the day.

Outside of work, find a hobby that is fulfilling. You may even find that time spent on the hobby will prompt inspiration. When you relax, you will start to dream again. The most effective way to avoid burnout is to find joy away from work.

A successful leader knows that employees are more productive and creative when they avoid burnout as well. Part of building relationships with team members includes genuine concern for their well-being. Let them know that their emotional and physical health is a priority.

> ➤ Question for Thought: What programs do you have in place to help employees with their physical, financial, and emotional health?

> ➤ Action Step: Set aside 15 minutes for yourself each day to recharge.

Tip #19: Keep the Big Picture in Mind

A leader's job inherently involves putting out small fires and dealing with unexpected complications. The most efficient leaders are able to prepare for the next step even while addressing urgent issues day-to-day. Be prepared to navigate your team through changing circumstances by keeping an eye out for new opportunities. Frequent communication is essential in change. Including colleagues in transitions eliminates the fear of the unknown and increases productivity and motivation.

A good way to evaluate whether or not you are keeping the big picture in mind is to take a look at how you spend your time. If you are spending most of your time on things that are urgent but not important, you may be losing sight of the overall vision.

True leaders inspire others by first inspiring themselves; their passion is evident to those around them. Make your mission a personal priority. Step back to view the big picture and then make any adjustments necessary to keep your team on track. Remind yourself what fuels your passion and why this work matters.

> ➤ Question for Thought: What is on your calendar this week? This month? Does the way your time is scheduled accurately reflect your priorities?

> ➤ Action Step: Identify the next big step for your company or yourself.

Tip #20: Try New Things

Never be satisfied with being static. True leaders who inspire lasting change are those who recognize that innovation is key to long-term success. When you demonstrate a willingness to try new things, team members will feel encouraged that the company is not stuck in a rut. If you find fear of failure interfering, refer back to Tip #1.

Keep reading, learning, and looking for new ideas. Be open to new experiences. Albert Einstein once said, "I am neither especially clever nor especially gifted. I am only very, very curious." By asking questions and staying curious, you will avoid complacency.

Be looking for new ideas. Learn about how things work. Use the things you discover and are interested in as you continue to dream. Stay inspired so you can continue to inspire others.

> Question for Thought: When was the last time you took a chance on something new?

> Action Step: Find something that ignites your curiosity and study it.

Conclusion

In order to inspire others and create profound visions that lead to progress, a leader must first understand why his or her work matters. Rather than starting with *what* you want to do or *how* you plan to do it, focus on *why* you feel passion for your project. Once you can answer that question, everything you do and say will radiate your vision. Your authenticity and enthusiasm will infect others with the same passion and lead to lasting progress. Making the most of these 20 tips, including the questions for thought and action steps, will empower you to articulate your profound vision and lead with confidence.